Praise for

The Art of Naming My Pain

"These pages, which offer sinew and pedagogy in the midst of visual art, prose and verse, make *The Art of Naming My Pain* both a vulnerable and fearless multi-genre collection. Richardson's art, experience, activism and care pierces from the page into the heart and consciousness of her readers. Her essays drip in the rawness and scholar of Lorde and Hemphill, and the poems and visual work are like contagious candy to readers' eyes and ears."

— avery r. young, author of *neckbone: visual verses*

"Richardson's deeply personal and transgressively honest writing on mental illness will inspire and encourage others to liberate themselves from the stigma that has never belonged there in the first damned place. It is one of the many jewels in this book to be treasured."

— Magdalena Gomez, performance poet, playwright and author of *Shameless Woman*

"Richardson has broken down every trope and cliché of the Bildungsroman and replaced it with a narrative that is searing, remarkably original and startlingly beautiful. Telling her story as a queer Black woman and mother, and giving witness to her travails in the mental health system, Richardson has done more than made a way out of no way. She has alchemized her way into enduring literary art."

— Robert Lashley, author of *The Homeboy Songs*

"This is a book of stunning bravery and beauty. Richardson reminds us of Frida Kahlo in the way she's perfected the deep inward gaze. Readers will feel as if they know Richardson as she describes moments of mental illness, racism, and feeling awkward in one's body. But, she assures us 'it's much less lonely in the dark than you think' and by the end, when she writes 'we are dancing anyhow,' that's exactly how the reader feels."

– Renee Simms, author of *Meet Behind Mars*

"With lyric grace and searing vulnerability, Kellie Richardson generously offers us insight into how an artist can make – create and name – her way through the painful geographies of contemporary America."

– Tamiko Nimura, writer

"*The Art of Naming My Pain* is testament to the power that we (re)claim when we name all of our selves. This is a work that charges us to face our own hearts while becoming familiar with Richardson's. With each painting, essay, and poem, we are gifted the affirmation that beauty coexists alongside its many antonyms, and that we can be both bruised and brave."

– Thy Nguyễn, poet and community organizer

"*The Art of Naming My Pain* is a powerful second act to Richardson's first book of poetry, *What Us Is*. From the brilliant first essay, which critiques the common and not-so-critically-engaged assumptions about 'safe space' to her vulnerable and self-empowering exploration of what's wrong with institutions meant to heal mental health … to the uplift of 'Love Wins,' you won't want to miss the journey and truths Richardson offers us through her words and art. This is a must-read for everyone interested in the power of words, the power of the visual, and the liberatory power and redemption in the call for all of us to continue to refine and reignite our individual and collective commitment to social justice."

– Shelli Fowler, Associate Professor, Virginia Commonwealth University

"In *The Art of Naming My Pain*, Richardson not only names but calls out and takes to task her pain – Black pain, Mother pain, Woman pain, Queer pain – and its sources. Her words and art are charged with a pulse that resonates along a scale holding humor as well as fear, delight as well as anger. In an era that feels more dangerous every day, *The Art of Naming My Pain* reminds us that we are not alone as we navigate through the darkness."

– Lydia K. Valentine, poet and playwright, *Aliquippa*

The Art of Naming My Pain

By Kellie Richardson

Blue Cactus Press | Tacoma, Washington

Cover art: "Listen" by Kellie Richardson

Cover design by Sam Tait

ISBN: ISBN-13: 978-1-7330375-1-8

ISBN-10: 1-7330375-1-9

Blue Cactus Press | Tacoma, Washington

To Patricia, Jaeda, and Zion – no one understands us. Not even us. And that's everything.

To Annie – for teaching me the ecology of friendship.

To ALL the brilliant Black girls who never really fit in.

Table of contents

A Warning: The Subjectivity of Safe Spaces / 1

The Art of Naming Your Pain / 7

Summertime / 13

When the White People Ask Me How I'm Doing / 27

Set / 33

How I Learned to Leave / 39

Punishment / 40

Daddy Lessons / 41

The Scar Below My Waist / 43

Baby Girl's Dream / 45

First Born / 47

Assurance / 49

Untitled / 50

Church Dinners / 51

Haiku / 53

Untitled / 57

Just Say No / 63

Black Girl's Guide to Voluntary Commitment / 71

Sick / 87

Alone / 90

Clear and Present Anger / 91

Search / 92

Spring / 93

Avery Young Loves Me ... He Just Don't Know It Yet / 94

Remember / 97

Love Wins / 100

A Warning: The Subjectivity of Safe Spaces

A ship in port is safe, but that is not what ships are for. Sail out to sea and do new things.

– Grace Murray Hopper

As an educator and organizational consultant, I can't tell you how often I hear the term "safe space." Although much of the foundation of the term is associated with the LGBTQ community, educators and leaders love to apply it to diversity, cultural competency and equity work. Folks are always referring to creating, establishing, or protecting safe spaces in the interest of those considered marginalized, underserved, disadvantaged or any other term that conveys deficiency. I am a proponent of cultivating unapologetic community and belonging in my classrooms or any other teaching/training space I facilitate. However, I think what some people fail to realize, or even worse accept and endure, is that safe space for those you serve (whether students, community, peers, whatever) means a willingness to feel unsafe yourself. I don't mean unsafe as in subject yourself to violence or any form of blatant disrespect. I mean that if we really take the time to unpack this concept of a space in which safety is expected and defended on behalf of the collective, there is an inherent assumption of interdependency.

1

As such, the leader, be it teacher, CEO, or otherwise, connects, responds to and is driven by the rest of the group. There is a sharing of power; a leveling of authority. And this is where safe space can either be a bridge for transformation and authenticity, or another cruel ruse in leadership. Real safety results in folks bringing their whole selves – slang, physical expressions like dap and laughter, body language like sitting on the floor or looking down, and best of all THEIR specific truths; truths that often contradict or agitate the reality of the facilitator. In response, leaders rush through an important moment, a tipping point or point of clarification to preserve their own comfort levels. This turns the educator/leader from a gardener to a gatekeeper. Rather than trusting the nature and knowledge of the group, the scared leader shuts it down, and redirects the conversation to a less scary, more familiar place. The hardest demonstrations of this misstep occur when facilitators or professors brush over or discount a student's dissenting voice: a life experience that disputes statistics, an expression of offense, or my favorite...the raised voice of a Black student.

Safe spaces should be quiet sometimes. Individuals and groups need to marinate, think and reflect to reach or maintain differing conclusions. Learning is about engaging with difficult information and thoughtfully developing perspective on an issue. Silence is key to inviting everyone in to contribute in their way and time. The pressure to fill the silence robs this so-called "safe space" of truth. Truth, especially a truth that has been suppressed or silenced, is not often arrived at quickly or with force. Therefore, whoever is up front must be willing to 1) weather the discomfort of a slow, sometimes very quiet process; and 2) face the sting that the safety and subsequent input of others can bring.

If, as an educator or leader, you merely exist to ensure peace is maintained, or to present your take on a topic, without a commitment to invite the voice of others (many of whom might just have relevant insights to deepen the discussion) then you are party to a major downfall of today's discourse: one-sided pontificating that perpetuates a canon that denies the credibility, and sometimes very existence of "others." The current tragedies and protests have generated round after round of talks of allyship and what those in power can do. This is always a good conversation to have but folks must understand that safe space is a subjective term. What feels safe for you might be terrifying for others, and a great way to model your commitment to listening is to be willing to be clueless, vulnerable and downright scared. Settling in to the discomfort sends a message that your service to the whole outweighs your determination to be right or remain outside the need for safety. If you don't know how to shut up and take in the hard truths, you ain't about safe space. You diminish the validity and meaning of "safe space" if no one feels safe but you.

This book is a walk through my safe and unsteady space. May we all be equally terrified and redeemed.

"Listen" (2019). Acrylic, tissue paper, found items collage on canvas.

NEVER
ALWAYS **OK**
GOTABE

YES
NO
AYBE
SO

EADV
XPLIC

FREE AINT FREE

I disagree with those that think truth lies in the light. Truth evades me in the light. Pain sustains stealthily in the light because many gateways to truth are found and crossed in the darkest corners of our lives. I am consistently encountering people, tasks, messages and thoughts that are in direct opposition to the truth. Let me take a moment to define what I mean by "the truth" to offer some clarity. To me, truth is not a single experience or transcendence to a place other than here. It is not a destination or a souvenir you bring back from a faraway place. Truth is a meeting of soul and brain; one that illuminates your purpose. Truth brings both liberation and precision to small steps and big decisions. Truth is coming home to a house you built before you were born. It is rooted in our bones and released by what the elders call "a made-up mind." Truth is a lens through which I have come to see why I poison myself with comparison and seek happiness outside of myself. Damn, I hated writing that; felt like going to the grocery store without my bra on. But it's the truth. That's another way to define it, I suppose: truth is an expression of the realities and impact of your lived experiences; one that lends itself to your wholeness.

For some time, I believed that my truth was defined by the activity around me; that the world happened to me and truth was my response to it. I pivoted my state of being, my mood, even my outfit in response to external stimuli. It was painful but I didn't recognize it as such. I normalized it as the way it was; for me, for lots of other working women, for those of us "on the grind." I existed on in a space adjacent to my truth. Why? Because I was in pain. But I couldn't name it.

Good and happiness and joy were like water off a duck's back to me. My face smiled but my insides remained. Successes at work, happy hour meet up's, even both kids gone for the weekend did not eliminate a sense of heaviness. The light – the daylight, the day-to-day life – allows the luxury of my senses. Light helps me hide in errands and obligation; cling to movements of routine and aversion. My pain made me restless and afraid of sundown, afraid of the dark. For a time, I slept on the couch despite a perfectly good bed because I feared what waited for me beneath my eyelids. Ghosts of the past and present can be all-consuming. Sitting with myself was more than I could bear. My heart was congested with unexpressed and unexperienced pain. I felt it in my joints and my gut. Even my laughter was laced with a sour sadness. I watched shows, read books, googled this, that and the other just to find myself back at me. It was like a super Black and unfunny version of Groundhog Day. I caught myself side-eyeing those women who presented as happy and positive. That was a pretty low point as I pride myself on lifting others (particularly other women) up. I had to entertain the possibility of nothing changing. What if I stayed this way? Was I willing to watch the world expand and evolve while I stayed, shrunken and terrified in the dusty corners of my mind? I was signing up to become another bitter bitch that fed off others' insecurities and let my gifts go rancid in service of fear. Naw.

As a writer I believe in the power of language, the power of assigning meaning to something otherwise elusive. Language helps us navigate the world as a tool to share experiences with others. At our most innocent, we look to our caregivers to tell us what, why, how – we need them to name what's around us so we can see our way through and to what's next. I forgot to name my pain. Or maybe I never learned it. I denied myself the permission to feel it. I owed myself more. I had to make it right. I had to turn off the lights.

When you walk into darkness, other sensibilities must take over. It's disorienting and scary at first. Because of that we often scramble to turn the lights on. The weight of the fear does not seem worth the risk. You forget what could be gained by enduring the risk. If you choose to stay in the dark just one more moment, then one more moment after that, then just one more, you'll notice your hearing becoming sharper as you try to predict what is around you. Your eyes adjust. I could begin to name my pain.

I'm sad.

I'm afraid.

I'm confused.

I'm humiliated.

I'm lonely.

Your sense of touch gets keen as you stumble into things you know are there but aren't sure exactly what they are. When you hit an object, you must use your hands to gain clues. And without fail, a shape or slope, or maybe a texture will trigger a landmark you once passed, the scene of the crime, the source of the pain.

My mother's hands.

My lover's mouth.

My father's feet.

The monkey bars against my back. The blond hair flipped in my face.

The back against my wall. His hands around my neck.

Your flight reflex will kick in again, but if you stand your ground there in the dark, you allow yourself an opportunity to relive and examine those hurtful moments, the destructive decisions. You can give language to the feelings that stand between you and healing.

Stupid bitch.

I fucking hate your ass.

You've ruined your life.

You missed your chance.

That's what you get.

Find it, feel it and name it.

Shame.

Hurt.

Loneliness.

Abandonment.

Fear.

Longing. It's not an exercise in torment, it's your way home. Sit still in your darkness.

Feel your way.

Cry.

Scream.

Do whatever is on the other side of release.

Ask or offer forgiveness.

Visit the place to which you vowed to never return.

Be willing to eat your words.

Ask for what you need.

Do not apologize.

A lightness of being is cool but happiness is rarely an unearned privilege. Black women in particular must cling to and stand in our truth with titanium boots in a safe house built by Jesus Herself. Our ankles swell, our backs sway and shake, and it hurts. And I will give voice to this pain. I will name my pain to honor myself, to center my humanity in a world that doesn't. I don't wait for permission. I close my eyes and find the words. It's much less lonely in the dark than you think.

There were so few times when all four of them were together. Pity this memory would almost ruin it.

"There's a special vibration to being Black," his mother explained earlier that year. "There are sensibilities that you have inherited from me, from your dad, from relatives even I never met or don't remember. It's how we have stayed around. Because we are keen to what's around us, what's to come. We feel stakes get high, we sense a new person in the room. We find each other in a sea of strangers so we know where to turn if it gets dangerous. We don't turn our backs to the door of the restaurant. We face what's coming even when we have no clue what's coming. It's how we are still here."

Jay found it downright weird that his mother would even bring up his father. They split up years ago when Jay was just a little kid. Fast forward to his mother marrying a woman. Jay had no idea how what seemed to be an extreme change of heart came to be; how a perfectly good life gets reset into an okay one with more square footage and less soda in the fridge. But it had. He was the youngest person in the house with the least privilege. And his brother was leaving for school soon so he would really be on his own.

Do you need a dad to show you how to be a man? he thought. Immediately, he felt bad for the annoyance he felt toward his mother. He would never tell her that she was cool and that he loved her. Even though he did. But the closeness he felt toward his mother didn't soothe the edge in his walk or his demeanor. It didn't soften his sullen way of making his lunch and folding his laundry (it wasn't even totally dry yet). He was resentful of every new ritual he had to master like wake-up times and loud lady parties. His mom was still his mom, but in this house, she was brighter and charged with a pulse he couldn't identify. She was still sarcastic and focused on tasks and her word games. She still danced to hip hop while she cooked and made a cocktail as soon as she came home from work. But in this house, she was less asleep. Or maybe she was more awake? Either way, Jay saw his mother's skin a little bronzer, her full lips were glossier. Even first thing in the morning. It was like someone wiped her down with Armor All and the dust was gone.

A flash of light from the front window drew him out of his head space. It was the familiar blue and red flicker of authority. Jay could not remember a time he didn't recognize and respond to the presence, or even the potential, of the police. This was the vibration his mother talked about. He hated it. It felt like a curse, a burden, a recurring rash that only Black folks got.

Jay's mothers were upstairs. They were always upstairs. Shuffling, laughing, trading words and changing channels. He and his brother, Cory, were scrolling through movie options but had not agreed on what to watch. The whole process was dumb really, because they always ended up watching their favorite movie. They knew the beginning, the middle, the end, all the supporting characters, the outfits and punchlines of the main characters. They'd seen it a thousand times but weren't the least bit tired of it. Sometimes predictability is a comfort. Even to a teenager.

He saw his brother's long, grasshopper legs straighten as he rose from the couch to part the blinds with his fingers. The same long sienna fingers that thumped him in the back of the neck and cracked open sweaty cans of soda at the park.

"Who they got now?" Cory asked, although it was really more of a declaration that the ritual was about to begin. Jay's muscle memory took over and he followed Cory out onto their porch to bear witness.

This is how you know summer has officially begun. It's not the smell of sun in your stuffy nose, or peaches in the produce section. It is officially summer when the cops shake you down before your mom even turns on the stove to start dinner.

Apprehension and curiosity grew stronger and spread from Jay's chest to his stomach and ears. His inclination was to run but to where and why? He was already at home and running out of the house was a damn foolish move. He glanced over to see Cory recording the whole thing on his cell phone. The boy across the street. On his knees. Then down on his stomach. His jeans fit big, like Jay's – his mom always bought them large so they'd last through the school year – so they had sunk a little too low beneath his waist, exposing his black underwear. Jay wore that brand, too.

"Don't you move," the cop said. He didn't yell it or scream it the way some police did. He used the same tone Jay and Cory used on each other when they were playing video games. It was arrogant and mocking with the cruel amusement of a hunter in the woods. The hunter who sees his unknowing prey through the sights of his gun.

The boy was not moving and knew better than to try. Every limb was as still as his frightened breath would allow. He didn't say a word. He only seemed to wait for instruction, hoping not to miss what was required of him. He wore a simple white t-shirt, the kind that come in packs of 3 and last Jay a semester before the armpits started to get yellow. How come that never happened to his moms' shirts, he wondered.

"Mom!" Cory's voice snatched Jay's attention.

"Mom, come here and bring your phone!"

Although he was directing his request upstairs, Cory kept his direction forward, his phone steady in his hand as he continued to record.

Jay heard the thump of feet descending their short flight of stairs. Well, there were actually three flights. Their house was built about a hundred years ago in a style that was characteristic of their neighborhood. Theirs was a common landing place for

Italian immigrants in the early 1900's. Homes big enough for budding families toting a grandparent, but small enough to afford the dismal prospects of employment that awaited unwelcomed newcomers. Small enough that you could call out to anyone in the house and they could hear it. Small enough that it didn't take long to escape from the back. Small enough to plant fig trees that, when they grew tall, would give you both privacy and provision. Small enough to build a dream on.

Jay could always smell his mom before he saw her. The tea tree in her hair and the amber soap she showered with let him know he could anticipate her entry at any moment. He had learned to long for and dread that smell.

"What's crackin'?" his mom asked as she opened the door to join them on the porch. "Oh. Okay then."

That last statement meant she didn't really require a response. She simply sighed. Jay saw her light dim and her eyelids tighten to take in the scene. She walked out as far she could without falling off the front of the porch. She was noting details: how many officers, what they looked like, trying to make out badge numbers from far away. She began recording what she saw in her phone like a chemist testing a hypothesis. The moment she had finished she stepped back and pulled Jay close to her.

"Stay here," she instructed.

Jay had heard this more times than he could count, and he knew to concede. It held the tone of a first responder dragging bodies from the fire and prying screaming babies from their dead mother's arms. It was critical and emergent. It was life or death. It was how she tried to keep her boys alive.

Jay's other mom, Lisa, had joined them on the porch and had already began recording on her phone. Her body was taut and alert in a way Jay rarely saw because she was the chill parent. They shared jokes and made fun of mom's anal ways. She snuck him a sip of beer once at a barbecue. Lisa meant business but her love for her family was all over her like her skin: soft, persistent, and everywhere.

Once filming a shake down begins, the dimensions of time slow down. It always reminded Jay of when his moms forced him to go to a museum. You walk up on a piece and you are supposed to stare at something you don't understand until it's time to move on. He was always grateful when there was an exhibit of something he could recognize. He felt like the other stuff wasn't made for him. It was another lecture imposed on him by someone he'd never met. He got enough of that at school.

He heard the boy on the floor cough. Then he sneezed and coughed again. Blades of grass jolted up and out with the gust of air that escaped his nose and mouth. Jay could tell he was afraid that his sudden movements would mean punishment. Or worse.

"I got allergies!" he shouted, as an apologetic explanation. "It's just allergies. I ain't resisting. I ain't gonna do nothing."

"We watching, bruh!" Jay heard his chill mom say. "We watching and it's going to be okay."

"Mind your own business, ma'am," one of the officers said without breaking his stance. "We know what we are doing."

There were now three guns drawn on the boy. There was the first officer on the scene: lithe, olive skinned, clean cut and a regular on Jay's block. He was always patrolling the residential streets as if issuing a warning (to whom no one knew). He was the kind of cop that was everywhere and nowhere. His service was purely theoretical, his role as protector was an inference made only by those who'd never met him. The second officer, Jay had seen at his school concerts because his daughter played on the drumline, too. He was the shortest, the fattest, and the least comfortable with Black people. Jay knew Black people made this dude uneasy because he was the one they sent to school assemblies to talk about drugs and safety. After the lectures he always went straight over to the principal and clung to him like a blanket until the students were released back to class. The third officer reminded Jay of a superhero. He was all sharp edges and angles. Even his face seemed to have a crease down the middle. He was new to the area and clumsy in who and how he interacted with people in the neighborhood.

The fact that he was even nervous at the gentrified coffee shops made Jay's mom say Black folks better stay clear of him.

Three cops, three guns, six arms extended and flexed. Three hands holding three fingers on three triggers. And one boy sprawled across a yard with his underwear showing.

Jay decided in that moment to start wearing the belt his mom had bought him.

Although each of the officers had gotten out of their respective cars, they had left the lights going. The block was blue and red and black and white and alive with worry. Those lights alerted the block to assume the position they normally took in times of war. You either come out or you bury yourself inside. Those that come out had already experienced the worst or knew they would soon, nothing to preserve or lose. They operate with the certainty of doom and surrender; it wasn't if, it was when. And so, they didn't avoid it anymore. Those who stayed inside put their hope in the power of good, the wisdom of authority, the bliss of denial. They worked to keep the neighborhood council from becoming the neighborhood watch, and they often urged everyone to keep their eyes on the prize.

By this time several neighbors were out. They were on their phones as well: recording, texting, trading predictions of the outcome. Jay worried about the outcome, too. He had learned about how things can turn from annoying to unbelievable in a matter of minutes. He understood the tectonic shift of brief moments in time. The four hours that Mike laid in the street. The eleven times that Eric said he couldn't breathe. The 11 months in court just for Philando's killers to go free. The hour or two Jordan spent at that house party before he was shot.

His youth, his innocence, made him put the outcome on pause in favor of determining that the present had the possibility to make this better; for this boy, for Cody, for him. Fear was an everyday accessory he wore like the bracelet his dad had given him for his 13th birthday. It rarely came off and when it did, you could tell the sun and school and sports and sleepovers had to work around it. It left a tan line: caramel underneath, earth all around. Fear changed his appearance. Fear changed the way his physical body showed up in the world. He hated taking the bracelet off because then everyone could see the mark fear had left on him. Scary bears don't get no respect.

His bracelet was on today though. Maybe, he thought, he could get a little bit closer. He could catch the eye of the officer whose daughter he played drums with. He'd have to remember me, Jay determined. He'd recognize me and see that me and the boy on the ground aren't that different. He'd remember how nice I am and how his daughter and I are cool. He'll step back and see that three officers, three arms, three hands and three fingers on three triggers is too much. Even if he did think black boys were trouble. Even if he did say *nigger* in his home around his friends and family.

Jay stepped away, or rather out, of his mother's arm toward the steps of the front porch. He felt a conviction within him drawing him to seek out and inform. Who he aimed to inform and what he'd say to do, he had no clue. But he did know that he wanted his say.

"Jay. Jay! Jay, get back up here!" his mom hissed. Her demand was urgent and pointed because she knew how this could end.

And Jay knew, too. But he now knew something else. Or rather, he remembered. He remembered the basics of arithmetic. He remembered three (cops, arms, hands, triggers) were always going to be more than one. He remembered how long it took his mom to get Cody to talk about getting questioned by security at the mall last summer. He remembered that there is a special vibration to being Black. He remembered to face what's coming so he could survive. So they could all survive.

Jay's mom grabbed Cody's arm to keep one of her boys close. Not further from harm mind you, just closer to her.

His other mom, Lisa, lowered her arm to stop taping. She followed Jay off the porch. Her pace mimicked his closely but at a measured distance that was at once protective and expectant. She fully intended to match and then exceed Jay's pace so she could step in front of him and turn him back toward the house. This was not the time for bravery, she thought. Loyalty lost black boys their lives. Pride was more expensive than any of the games these boys begged for at holidays or the shoes they grew out of monthly.

The crunchy fuzz of the police radio was the only element breaking up the congestion and silence. It was intermittent and unexpected, similar to its owners.

Lisa's calves drove the balls of her feet to quicken her step. Her left foot had just edged out Jay's right foot when she saw the chunkiest of the cops lower his gun and yank the boy up by his jeans saying, "Go on, then. Go on about your day."

Jay saw the other two officers drop their weapons. He saw their tactical belts struggle against their guts. They were still breathing heavy but relented in their stance as if they had just finished a race and won. Jay is sick of them winning.

Everyone stopped cold. Jay held the warm air he had just inhaled in his chest so he could try and understand what was happening.

The boy remained standing with his hands up. Dead grass covered the front of his shirt and jeans. Grass was stuck to the left side of his face from his chin to his forehead, still wet with sweat and confusion. Grass was caught in his eyelashes, and his glasses had been forced off center from being on the ground so long. He was on his feet but he wasn't moving. How could he know it was really over? How could he trust it wasn't a trick so the gunshot would be in his back? So it looked like he was running away.

Jay heard Cody talking into his phone to offer his followers commentary.

"They lettin' him go, y'all," Cody said. "Just like that. They lettin' him go."

The cop repeated himself. "You hear me? We know it ain't you. Go 'head and be on your way."

The other two officers were headed back to their vehicles exchanging farewells laced with collegial play and fun, fraternal mocking. The big one gave the boy one last, "Go on home. It's over." The relief of unrealized threat and the heat moved him to slide his hat off of his head. The hair that was left on his head clung to his scalp like shreds of seaweed at low shore. The parts of his scalp that were bald were shiny blotches of freckled tan and pale pulsing pink. There was a dent where his hat used to be, and he had a hearing aid in his right ear. He slipped his gun back in its holster and shifted his belt up over his gut, taking a deep breath.

The boy, still unsure and stationed on the yard where he was laid out just moments before, glanced ever so slightly to his right. Jay's gaze met his inquiry.

Jay understood and immediately nodded in response. The boy's shoulders relaxed, and his hands lowered until his arms were all the way down. His breath slowed, not in relief but in grief. The boy knew he had made it to the other side of this thing, and now was the time to find somewhere to put it. He would make it home today. He would stay in tonight. He would text his girl when he got home.

He took a first step and then another until his gate straightened and his pace reached a rhythm that Jay and Cody and their moms recognized as their own. As the boy walked, Jay saw him brushing the grass off of his shirt, his pants, picking it out of his hair. The boy straightened his glasses and Jay heard him begin to hum. Jay immediately recognized the tune because the video had just dropped yesterday and it had gone viral. A summer anthem, they were calling it.

Jay heard the boy snceze as he rounded the corner.

When the White People Ask Me How I'm Doing

What I want to say is – well, actually, I don't even want to respond. I want to pretend I can't even see them. Or maybe that I can't speak English. I don't want to be bothered. But if I were to respond sans filter, I would say:

My heart and spirit are bruised for the constant disregard of my people's lives. Their very existence proves to be of no consequence not only to the powers that be, but from everyday people who are our neighbors, teachers, and so-called friends. People that click the sad face emoji on the social media post that announces another Black death, transgender murder, state violence acquittal, but never a comment. People like you.

Perpetual stories of murder strip me of the motivation for pleasantries. My senses are heightened in search of redemption, of unleaded air I can breathe. Even more painful – and I am using the word PAINFUL here to stress to you, White person, that this is not about my anger, justifiable aggression and hostility....nope, this is about the pain I'm in; the ache with which I move through this office. It HURTS. The hurt festers and turns to rage, but racism's first strike is painful. A systematic dismantling of my dignity, our potential, our humanity; I am no longer human, I am a manifestation of the oppressor's hoarding of power and control.

Okay, back to my original point. What is so painful is that these crimes remind me that nothing I do, accomplish, contribute or intend is of any importance. My black body, face, and presence is always a negative. I am never welcome, and I am never wanted. Ever. Even when I thrive, someone White, must remind me of my inferiority, or that my accomplishments are the result of the oppressor allowing or permitting it. Not that I earned it, deserved it or am worthy of success. My shit's just by chance or by generous gift. And worst, a pathology of fear torments and taunts, driving us to equip our babies with battle plans and exit strategies instead of tools of possibility and real promise. Before you scurry off, let me just say that my son is fifteen. Long ago, he learned to step lightly and be undetectable by police. He has already been victimized racially at school (when he was six no less), and his parents' advice will always be imbued with the nuances of keeping his ass alive, out of jail, and unscathed by systemic racism, or worse yet by White folks that ask him how he's doing but don't really care to know. And this is the journey of Black parents. It is a real and enduring yoke that we are collateral damage in America (and abroad), and that reality scrapes and agitates my sensibilities, even in the face of a good day. I won't go so far as to say, and still I rise, but I will say I choose to remain IN this world and not OF it.

I do not accept the world telling me to just be thankful. No, kindly don't forward me that TED talk you thought I'd like.

I choose not to be so busy buying up shit that I forget I still don't have what I really want.

I do not embrace the oppressor's perspective of my own people; nor do I rely on it for validation. Hearing you recognize how "cool" my hair is does nothing for me. You're late to that party.

I do not accept the media's assertion of who we are; only God is the author of my people's possibility.

My soul is alive, motherfuckers. And ain't no one killing it!

But when White people ask me how I'm doing, what I say is, "Oh hey, I'm good. You?"

"Unrested" (2017). Magazine clippings, acrylic, found items collage on canvas.

Tyshawn
Jamal
James
Tommy
Demetrius
Sincere
Eric
Trayvon
Tyre
Bianca
Alton
Carnell
Tamir
Keith
Korryn
LaQuan
Charles
Richard
Mike
Philando
Sandra
Freddie
Charleena
Jordan
Alfred
Walter
Terence

Set

Set.
Decided.
Grounded as a stone's belly.

I have been named!

Designated with steel resolve
and bloody whip
Before a crowd.
In a book.
On a slab.
In a laboratory of cruel strangers.
Before my mother's mother was a babe.

I am the supply bred for demand.
For beck and call.
For sport and feast.
For pontification and jest.
For leverage of the least.

You constructed me
from an economy of lust,
stripped me of agency,

assigned me the sole task
of function.

Work horse. Harvester. Pacifier.
Scapegoat. Wet nurse.
On call companion. On call mistress.
Carpenter. Blacksmith.

I was a fucking footrest!

Because of the labels –
Murder cloaked in science,
a taxonomy to support the sickness,
a cancer turned birth defect.

You selected me for submission
to interrogation.

Front. Side.
Laid out. Bent over.
Split open.
Spread eagle.
Restrained. Infected.
Observed. Probed.

To identify, classify, specify
the root of my inferiority;

to rationalize a brutality
so utterly shameful
your offspring refuse to claim it.

You found my predisposition
to endure,
an orientation towards servitude,
without considering it was God's gift
and not yours.

Jettisoned my humanity to feed
your allure for dissection,
rationalizing depravity
in the interest of public good.

It's them labels.

Designations free from spirit,
fueled by White power plays
that still slice this earth
like I once sliced sugar cane
baby asleep on my back.

I conceded. We conceded.
My feet remain soaked
in the labels.

I step softly in and out of
the boxes you've created
to spare myself pain,
spare myself lashes.

Stay out the hot box.
Keep breathing.
Stay awake.
Stay woke.
So persistent and acute is
the pathology of your qualifiers
My great great great grandchildren will
own the compass through this land.

They too will walk
through the minefield
of your labels.

Those god damned labels!

They are born to yearning;
the bastard child of desperation.
You put a word behind the wheel,
declared it law
drove my legacy into a homespun
springboard for separatism.

The labels have taught your children
entitlement to me
and to mine –
My thoughts, my body, my prayer.
My hope, my dance, my hair.
As if my pilgrimage from
Mali to Maputo
to Middle Passage to Mississippi to Mobile
to Missouri to Minneapolis to Miami
is a story woven for your consumption.

You always sit at the center.
Feeding on me.
Just feeding on me.
This is not behind you or I.
This is still us,
this addiction to labels
for the good of
the pale and favored.

We have settled
into the grooves
of this dimension.
We live in deference
to the labels.
The seduction of security
restricts and relents

able hearts from disrupting,
from choosing
to know me outside of the labels.

Freedom can't ring
in a house of lies.
You can't taste my truth
in a big bowl of conditions.

We will roar and ring around this clock again
and again, and again and again,
because the profession of love
doesn't really matter when
what you say ain't what you mean.

Freedom is choice
that manifests
in self and wealth.
I don't need your privilege
to navigate my own.

Freedom is a life
without labels.

This piece was inspired by Carrie Mae Weems' *From Here I Saw What Happened and Cried.* I offer this in deep respect and gratitude to her conviction to bear witness to the Black experience.

How I Learned to Leave

I am the cold comfort of night.

I procure light
from distracted stars,
so that I may appear
to be less dangerous.

I am the impenetrable promise of home.

I am wolf and vanguard
taking my rightful place
as muse and messenger;
it has already been decided.

I am warm wind on cold skin.

I resent and repeat your precious lies,
pose as passenger, learning to drive myself
from hell to bright blue sky.

Punishment

She choked me.
Her soft hostess hands
couple to exorcise

a demon from my neck,
which she says is too long
for a child so short.

Under the pressure,
my mosquito bites burst,
wet and defeated.

Paideia.

Body flush to the wood paneling –

cold back. hot head. stupid girl.

My overalls grew tight, breath held.

I wanted to please her –
        she made everything possible, prettier, correct –
but I have to learn.

Suffer.

Submit.

I don't even remember why.

Daddy Lessons

Yesterday,
 just after lunch,
I learned that my father
is just a man.

His edges are not steel.
His heart is average.
His love is flawed and self-serving.
Just like me.

He did little to prevent
my bitter discovery
because he had no idea,
I was even looking

through the mess
he always leaves,
behind my eyes
and in my belly.

There is no mirror
in his pocket
of snappy comebacks
and rustic Black wisdom.

I try and fail

to find myself
fought for –
I want more.

I don't know how
to be branded
and abandoned by
my very best friend.

The Scar Below My Waist

Aspirational lovemaking with a fool.

Unyielding nausea and a set
of 5 withdrawals on my transcript.

Meatloaf, mashed potatoes and milk
feed the parasite.

They said it was a girl.

Fluid. Induction. Settled in to the rural hospital
after taking my final exam (I passed).

Twelve hours of pushing and the little girl is stuck.

They dry shaved my crotch and buried yesterday in the bin
with the other dirty things.

Welcome, little lady bug.
I feel I should immediately apologize.

Smell of Pop's tobacco.
He dropped off his disappointment
on his way to play piano in Spokane.

"We don't get black girls in here," the nurse disclosed to no one.

That was the year that hip hop
cranked out classics,
my shame began to swell.

Campus air was hot and expectant,
the locals were all too happy to see us go.

We made love so maybe we really were in love.

Twelve hours of pushing shame and I am in love.
State assistance. Caregiver. Coupons.

Stop wasting time waiting; it's not coming, love.

Do you even remember how this all began?

Baby Girl's Dream

Truth or Dare is a dumb game.
Others find it exciting
but not me.

Because it's old news.

The truth is no matter
how many times you dare me,
I'm not tasting crab apples,
or nigger knocking on Crazy Miss Lady's front door,
or closing my eyes in the closet with Little Eddie.

And I won't ever dare to tell
the pale, scrunched up faces
on the way to school
that they scare me.

I will simply stay away.
And I'll keep my legs so strong
that my bike will whizz past them
before they can call the cops.

I'm gonna play basketball.
And I'm gonna win.

And when I save up enough,
I'm jumping off the porch
and I'm floating right up into
the big burning orange sky.

I'll look down on our block
and keep watch on other brown girls
with butterflies in their tummies,
and dreams they won't talk about.

I'll keep them safe.
Safer than me.
And we'll find each other
on the other side of the fence.

First Born

Your will is painfully
acute and I'm sure that
you will resent me for asking

But –

To what end is all this?
Your speech and comments
are wounds that read as
polished intention.

You have read and reiterated
all the rhetoric of personal peace
and diversion of device.

Your wit sharp and addictive,
your confusion tethered
to my regret.

I always marvel at what
I taught you without a word:

Pretty pride.
Lonely is luxury.
Move until you collapse.

I'm sorry I lied
and failed, but if
history is a teacher
we will both
come out fat and catty.

Assurance

There is a heart at the heart of you.
Burrowed within,
below prayers of kin,
under thickets of despair.

And she is waiting there.
With a message from her mother,
about the nature of untruths
and the quick pivots of fortune,
the devastation of family.

And I am there.
Clearing gutters and
planting flowers,
holding your fury
much closer than my own.

This is the walk.
These are the steps
toward each other,
toward the end.

And I am there,

Until the devil's done fighting.

Untitled

I have seen you. Raising heaven. Steaming with fever, furious with uncertainty. Shaking the twigs and dust of the wilderness out of your pressed trousers.

I have felt you. On balmy summer nights lightened only by the bitchy, teasing breeze. Dreamt petal soft and rose pink, settled in but always ascending. Under and over me, wedged between your hope and my passion, polished bright brown by twilight and laughter.

I have waited for you. In the lying arms of others, rocking apologetic babies to sleep. I squared up like a street soldier, ready to smash the shadows, but instead took them back to season the reasons I stayed.

I have killed for you. Murdered and exorcised a force destined to fail. Gutted a ghost blindfolded because you came; bearing my breath, shaming death for thinking you would lose.

I have died for you. Laid face down in disgrace before the fools who raised and debased me. Bones stripped of marrow, offering what done wasted. Shed my heart, my hair and my hell, just to be your baby.

Church Dinners

The combinations only we understand.
Cravings that were formed
before our grandmothers' tongues
formed in their fathers' mouths.

Fish teams up with spaghetti,
cabbage perched on the side.
There must be a roll.
They may run out of foil.

Salty, savory sours
soften the hours
of condemnation –
even the communion cups
are judging you.

We need food we can feel
in our elbows and hips,
the shit that licks our wounds
and burns our lips.

Lipstick on white plastic forks,
repressed and obsessed gets
finessed into sharp suits,
and under your dress.

The same lady that lost her wig
when the spirit was high
makes the cake you will
fight the big kids for.

And you will win.

Because everything else
feels like loss.
Better clean your plate.
You know we don't waste

nothing.
Not even the opportunity
to work for the blessing
that was yours

from the very beginning.

Haiku

She was disgusted
at the sight of anyone
loving me better

"Float" (2018). Acrylic, magazine clippings, found items collage on canvas.

Untitled

In the beginning, under the coffee table was always the safest place for me. My mother, an undiscovered ingenue in interior decorating, always found a way to obtain the most magnificent coffee tables. Massive, heavy, authoritarian even. The wood was dense and omnipotent. It knew what I needed and what threats surrounded me. Our coffee tables took on the role of protector, shelter, think tank, and imaginary friend. I was painfully shy and unwilling to engage with house guests. But I wanted to be "at the party" so to speak. So, I figured the best way to do that was to scurry on over to Club Coffee Table so I could feed off the energy of braver souls. I could hear grown folk business...sometimes. Black moms don't play about kids being nosy. My mother had a continuum of deciding what was okay for me to hear, and what I needed to be banished for. I didn't care. I just loved seeing brown, painted toes in Candie's platforms or ebony feet in jellies or canvas Mary Jane's you could get from the drugstore (back then it was Payless – not the Shoe Source ... an actual drug store).

It was fodder for my imagination. It filled in the apologies I was already making for myself to myself. For not being cool. For not having what the other white girls in the neighborhood did. For being a ballerina with a big booty. For being afraid as fuck. Like all the time.

In the beginning, I could do the splits, and I ran around barefoot from July to August. I went outside voluntarily. I rode a bike. I was super pumped to inherit my sister's bike which now that I look back was kind of tragic. BUT at the time I loved knowing that it was my turn to take on the neighborhood in what had once been Jewel's ride. Picture this shit:

Yellow banana seat. Airbrushed rainbow body. Plastic, multicolored ribbons coming out of the handlebars. Oh yes, I was indeed taking my place in the winner's circle. There was a declaration of freedom that happened when my little baby butt hit banana seat, bare feet pushed pedals, and the ride picked up its pace. Braids started bobbing, and once those ribbons started flying in the wind, it was on! I realize now one reason I loved those ribbons so much was because they could do shit that my thick, coarse hair couldn't. They blew in the wind the way I wanted my hair to blow in the wind.

Another reason I loved being at the party but not a part of the party was that it gave me the distance and freedom to watch my mother be this luscious, effortless hostess. When people were over, the fevered annoyance that I came to recognize as her default countenance was gone. There were virtually no signs of it. I never saw her snap at her guests the way she gouged my sister and I with volume and word choice. I never saw her snatch their hearts clean out of their chests with a laser hot stare and pointed finger. Her hands were soft, nails meticulously painted, carefully curated rings adorned that scary pointed finger. I never saw her present her guest with a homemade dessert crafted just for them, and then yell at them for requesting a specific piece of it – flashback to my second-grade birthday.

Nope. None of this happened. She simply glided around in a caftan or tube top (terry cloth of course) granting requests before they were even made. Cocktails, pigs in a blanket, explanation of her well laid collection of wicker baskets on the living room wall (or maybe it was the dining room?). My mom could present the abomination that was 1980's snacks like nobody's business. She could make wheat thins, cheez wiz and pimento look like art. She would even pick out the platter that complemented the color of the food. She was about beauty, aesthetic, and presentation. This is often what happens to women who haven't been afforded the opportunity to tap into and develop their natural gifts. They get funneled; reallocated really. So, rather than my mom going to Parsons, she created beautiful ensembles, spaces, and experiences in the space where she reigned supreme: her home. Every room was planned out. And no clearance rack or thrift store was left unexamined in pursuit of the look she had envisioned. There is no fury more intense than my mother bringing her vision to life. It's the way others build start-ups, or train for marathons, or how survivalists hunt for wholesale nonperishables. It only makes sense to the individual that has the vision, right? Scouring fabric scraps to make fly ass pot holders or trivets. Re-imagining a bathroom as a destination versus just a room to go pee. It was like she had a supernatural ability to spot, secure and transform shit other people had deemed unusable, irrelevant or expired.

Mom had a temper though...and a razor tongue. She caught my big sister making out with a dude at the local skating rink. I watched in horror as she read her for filth right there in front of everyone. It would take you months to regroup and accumulate the nerve to think you were worth a damn. Again, supernatural. I don't think this is specific to my mother though. Especially now that I have my own kids. I recognize (usually on the back end) how easily I can obliterate them with my words. Or even my lack of words. Hell hath no fury like a mother's silence. It is dense, and unyielding and full of messages that send you on a shame spiral of self-doubt, rage, regret, resentment, and disorientation. Just an utter mess. There is an art to how we tear each other to shreds. Whether we give or receive it, domestic terrorism within families is undeniable. And I am guilty of planting these seeds in my own kids. In my rare moments of optimism, I pretend that they will not damage their own children; that they will see the cycle, find the weakest points in it, blow it open and design a new way of being related. I pretend that the seeds are that of possibility, not poison.

But the sick side of me actually looks forward to witnessing them dishing out their unique brand of ugly – on their partners, their children, their close friends – because it will assure me that I'm not the monster I believe myself to be. I want to be assured I am deserving of their care as my body deteriorates, and that their care comes from a well of gratitude. I want them leaning forward, at the side of my bed, reading me Audre Lorde, praying for peace they believe I earned. I want to believe that I won't have to beg for their time, that I won't have to keep forgiving them for ignoring me. I want to believe that they don't fail me like I failed my mother. I really did fail her. And then I went and failed me.

Just Say No

I have got to learn to say no. Even to the people I love. ESPECIALLY to the people I love. I am friends with a White girl. A White woman. Like real friends. I wanted to make sure she knew I was true to my word. About friendship. About being friends. About reciprocity. About what happens when Black girls speak truth to White girls … about other White girls. I wanted to have a friendship be real to me and for me. I needed to reassure myself that trusting my heart to a White woman, to this White woman, was right and true.

I have taken prior chances on White women. I have trusted them with unedited personal stories. I have invited them into my home to hang out. I have trusted a few White chicks with my tears. Shortly after, I realized I was being used as a feather in their cap; a way to better understand Black culture. I had been cast as the Black girl sidekick in their White girl sitcom. And at the end of the show, I had served my purpose. They had taken what they could (insights into Black hair, practice using slang, advice on dating Blacks) and moved the hell on to the next adventure in race relations. I had been tokenized and discarded. Then I went through the process of chastising myself for not knowing better; for forgetting that there's only so far you are supposed to go with White folks. Especially White women. But my starry-eyed ass always wants to believe in possibility, in the reality of authentic relationship across race. Actually, not just across race. I want to believe I can have authentic relationships with White women. I think I want to believe in the universal solidarity of White women. I haven't factored White men into this dream because even my imagination has limits. Sorry Dr. King, I'm only human. All this to say I didn't totally want to say yes. But I did. I said yes. Because we are friends. Because I believe in trusting possibility and showing up for your friends.

I said yes to going to a comedy show. Laughing is fun, I figured. It's not as if I only like Black comics. Shit I just like to laugh. So, I said yes to going with my White friend to a White comedy show in a super White theater. What could possibly go wrong? I could slam two cocktails in the lobby, sit through the show, hopefully laugh a few times, and head on home. I also figured I'd hear at least a couple fun gay jokes as the comic was a lesbian, and I always appreciate the opportunity to bask in my queerness among a sea of straight folks.

My friend picked me up, we entered the theater, and headed directly to the bar. We sipped our cocktails, and to her credit, she thanked me for coming. At least three times. I saw what she was doing and assured her I wanted to accompany her as we hadn't hung out in a while and we both needed some laughs. Other folks were milling in the lobby. It was so White, y'all. I felt hypervisible the way Black folks do in super White spaces. As someone who's lived and worked in my city for years,

I knew I'd see some folks I knew, and I did. They were all folks from my work life so there were lots of surface conversations about kids and their upcoming spring break, weather, shit like that. But the common thread was variations of, "Oh my gosh! I'm so surprised to see you here!" This was my first concrete verification that this show probably wasn't gonna be for me. While I'm sure they were genuinely surprised to see me, there was another message beneath that statement. Know what I'm saying? I think you do.

We found our seats in the mezzanine. It was a full house. A super full, super White house. The chair was uncomfortable and so was the environment. I spend my whole week navigating spaces where I am one of the few Black folks in the room (sometimes the only), doing the mental Olympics of "*if I do this, then maybe this, and then that*," and "*nope, I'll do that instead.*" Or, most of the time, I opt out, do nothing and save my mental and emotional capacity for my actual job duties.

I realized quickly that this was not my kind of comedy. As I shifted periodically in my uncomfortable seat, I worked hard not to categorically write the whole show off as "White people humor." But it kind of was. References to Seinfeld and camping, annoying hipsters …things that just don't intersect with my lived experiences. It's not a value judgement, it's just a fact. But I was there with my friend. My White lady friend to whom I had actually grown close. So, I worked to stay positive and made the most of it. I listened for common ground. I recited Janelle Monae lyrics. I made a mental grocery list. I quieted the unapologetic old Black women that governs my soul in White spaces. Her name is Perlie. I gave her a cigarette and a shot of brown liquor to distract her through this searing weight of Whiteness on my shoulders. Perlie took the shot and nodded off long enough for me to stay the course. I was encouraged to see that my friend seemed less than impressed as well. And then it happened. The comic told a joke that referenced the KKK. The joke wasn't funny. It was in poor taste. I felt sick. The audience exploded in laughter. My friend and I looked at each other. No words were spoken. My ears got hot. Miss Perlie awakened from her nap and she wasn't happy.

"I told you 'bout going to places that ain't for you," she said. "Now look at you."

The comic was riding the audience's energy, moving on to her next joke. I officially checked out of the show and I reasoned with Miss Perlie to just give me a minute to steady myself before finding a graceful exit. I played out the eventual erosion of this friendship; how we'd "lose touch" after the awkward end to an evening out together; how our schedules got crazy and I seemed "more and more distant." She'd report how I never could or would tell her why I was annoyed at the KKK joke. *Here we go again*, I thought. *I should have just said no.*

Black folks are no stranger to paying for, attending, and sitting through meetings, conferences, shows, and experiences that go sideways out of nowhere. We navigate these situations with precision and keen sensibility. It's how we are still here. I guarantee you it has happened before your very eyes and you didn't even know it. Unless you are Black. If you're Black, I'm certain you at least picked up on the vibe. We are a tribe that senses, responds to and endures waves of distress and tension. When a race-based violation occurs, any myriad of reactions can occur from dead silence to table flipping. It's rarely this clean though. More often than not, it is a wave of emotional turmoil fraught with suppressed emotions, a comparative analysis of risk and return, and another heap of unexpressed pain to add to your collection.

I felt my friend's elbow nudge mine. I looked over at her.

"Fuck this," she said. "I can't with this bullshit. Let's get out of here and get a drink."

"I'm right behind you," I said, already resolved to order a vodka martini with a twist.

She grabbed her Kate Spade satchel and we bounced.

When we got to the bar, we didn't spend a ton of time unpacking it. There was acknowledgement on both our parts that it was not our scene. She expressed her disgust at the joke and the twilight zone fuckery of the show. It was unfamiliar territory for both of us. I didn't affirm her. She didn't apologize. Her words weren't driven by guilt and mine weren't centered on her comfort. I suppose that's why I don't have very many White friends. Friendship is about reciprocity and shared risk and burden on behalf of the other. Most of my would-be friendships with White women are predicated on my servitude to their egos and self-image. My experiences are for their consumption, sometimes it feels like an emotional autopsy. And when there's an opportunity for my White lady friend to "show up" in my defense, or better yet, for her to stop White led spaces from using me for their entertainment, or as evidence of their "wokeness," she falls silent. She leaves it to me to demand my dignity, to weather the storm while she sits in the car with the engine running. When I need them most, my former White "friends" still see me as other, less than and secondary to their need to be the center, the protected and the sacred. They can't shake the myth of their irrefutable innocence and honorable intentions. It's simply too hard to weather the sting of my Black truth: that I am human, beautiful and worthy of respect; that she has been party to a lie, wants to do better, but will continue to fuck up. I have experienced a willful resistance to the raw and painful truth of my experiences as a Black woman. Why would I offer my best self to this kind of dynamic? My trust of White women remains predictive. I believe that's the wisest way.

But Linda chose differently. Initiating our departure from a space that was unsafe and hurtful to me – without questioning me to validate her hunch, without requesting explanation or worse yet, ignoring and pretending nothing was going on – was a good moment. It was what I needed in the moment from my friend. I won't pretend that it has restored my hope in cross-racial friendships because it didn't. I still keep my circle small and I will likely always be distrustful of White women. I do, however, want to own my role in holding the White women that I know, with my truth. The truth is: I don't want to go to White comedy shows. My friends can handle me saying no. My friends value my happiness even when it displaces their comfort. I will continue to be honest and put myself first to chip away at the lie that White women need protecting or that their needs ever come before mine, especially in so-called sisterhood.

This story is not really a story. It's more of a guide. A travel guide of sorts. There's Frommer's and Zagat's. My story is kind of like that, if your travel plans include staying in the psych ward. This guide to voluntary commitment begins with Golf pencils. When someone asks what comes to mind after my brief stint in the hospital, that's my response: golf pencils. I never want to see another one. I likely won't have to since I don't play or even plan to play golf now or in the future. Either way, fuck golf pencils.

I lost my shit March of 2017. Now when I say lost my shit, I am referring to a dismantling of the connection between my body and mind; a severance between me and the world. I was no longer an actor. I was only a recipient. Of thoughts, of pain, of symptoms and wreckage. Nothing but contradictions: flurry and paralysis, fight and concession.

My breakdown was a mudslide of sorts. I call it a mudslide because 1) it was most certainly a natural disaster; and 2) a mudslide occurs when a large amount of water causes the rapid erosion of soil on a steep slope. And that, my friends, was like looking in a mirror. I was a disaster waiting to happen. The makings were always there, but I had managed to keep the precipitation and physics at bay. When it was getting too slippery, I frantically worked to dry out. Drying out in my case was isolation, withdrawing from everyone and everything, and escaping via words and images (books, writing, social media) to avoid my reality. When I had retreated enough to choke back the dangers of being found out, uncovered, questioned by those who truly know me, I would re-integrate, apologizing to those I had flaked on, put off, rescheduled, ignored.

Shame is the real driver for me. I simply hate my brain and its inability to function in everyday life. Function, independence, value-add, purpose; these are the qualities that lie at the center of my self-worth. And that was precisely the problem. Searching for self-worth outside of myself meant I would never find fulfillment.

Nothing could prepare me for the process of seeking medical help for my mental health crisis. No amount of research, anecdotes, or secondhand stories prepare you to be humiliated, dehumanized and disregarded by the system. Seriously, it's the shit that nightmares are made of.

ADMITTED

There is a stubborn shame that mental illness carries. It's so persistent that despite my insides burning from self-hatred, regardless of my complete inability to find a glimpse of relief, I resisted an admission of sickness. I tried to frame it as moodiness, PMS, fatigue, anything but what it is.

I feel like an alien among the rest of the population. I am an imposter, skillful though I may be, living for the sake of what I believe to be sheer obligation. A duty to support and sustain the world as my children, my wife, my family and friends know it. A world where I show up with productivity and purpose, where I help locate lost keys and jackets, where I am interested in their days, where the cabinets and freezer are stocked with snacks and dinner options. It is a covert operation with the sole purpose of invisibility. It's the least sexy or glamorous way to be a spy. Only I don't get the bad guy because I AM THE BAD GUY. I am the problem. Because I can't fix myself. I cannot reset my mind to "happy," or even content. I am literally living off excuses and living for the moments I can be in the dark with only my wicked, stupid self.

After days without sleep, the inability to sit still, the constant nausea, I first sought out my primary care provider to at least see if I could adjust my meds or find some immediate response to at least calm down and be able to sleep. My regular provider was unavailable, so I saw a doctor who had a same day appointment available.

My appointment was at 10 a.m. It was over at 10:15 a.m. Why, you ask? Because the doctor came in with his clipboard (while I was sobbing uncontrollably and mortified to even be in public), mumbled that I was on a really low dose and he'd call in a new prescription to double it. As I was trying to pull myself back together, he said to me, "Why are you crying? What's the problem?"

This humiliating and embarrassing question just made me more embarrassed and emotional. *You have my file, jackass...you know I'm here because I said I was in crisis.* Through snot and rage, I said, "I'm at a breaking point with my anxiety and depression. I can't function. I'm afraid. I need help."

To which he responded, "Oh. Ok. Well, I'll call in your meds. You can come back or call if you have questions."

And with that, he was gone. Outro. Ghost.

I remained perched on that cold exam table until the tears that were blurring my vision subsided. Any hope I had of addressing and treating my condition without it going public seemed impossible. Even worse, I truly believed the shame that would accompany exposing my breakdown would dismantle my life, kill my career, drive my children away, inspire those around me to pity me rather than love me. Who the hell would choose that route?

This is the point at which I shower myself in lies and delusion. They are in no way complicated or intricate. Super simple statements that reek of bullshit but allow me to cling to what I believe is my dignity. Here's a few highlights:

Bitch, you're fine.

If you put on a cute outfit and some makeup, your mind will follow.

Just get up. If you get out of bed, you'll be fine.

You don't have time to fall apart. You got shit to do.

What will the family say? You know they already think you are the weird one.

You're gonna fuck up the kids (even more).

And as I fed the fear, it grew. As I unpacked everything I hated about myself, it began to come out of my pores. Like a drunk, my body had had too much poison, and it worked to release it. But I kept feeding my demon more ammunition, I kept putting my powder keg of a brain closer and closer to an open flame.

My wife pushed me to allow her to be my advocate, and that we had to at least try to find help. Find help now. Right now.

We set out on a journey to secure treatment for me. A shaking, delirious, sobbing, insomniac asking for urgent help to keep her from hurting herself? Doesn't seem like an unreasonable request, right? WRONG. We spent the next 31 hours moving from Behavioral Health Walk-in, to Crisis Counselor, to Emergency Room. At the ER, I wasn't offered any form of medication to help me stabilize. The physician who came to "examine" me clearly didn't even want to touch me. She couldn't look me in my eyes, tapped some joints to check my reflexes, and then answered every request for info and help with, "We'll have to see what the social worker says." I checked in to the ER around 1pm on a Friday. I got a "light sedative" around noon on SATURDAY. I was out of my mind with sleep deprivation, the overall humiliation of having to recite again and again why I'm there (since it wasn't of a physical nature), and oddly enough, being told they're not sure I need commitment to a facility because I wasn't "suicidal enough."

Was this even real?

The overpaid doctor bitch couldn't wait to get out of my exam room. It's so very clear to me how someone having a mental health crisis just gives up and storms out of the ER. To go hide, go die. Because what's left by way of options? If the very place you are sent to "get help" demonstrates in no uncertain terms that not only are they afraid of you, but they'd just prefer not to be bothered by your innocuous problems, well then, what the fuck are you supposed to do?

Mental illnesses is glamourized by villains in thrillers and action films, and sensationalized by extensive true crime programming, but the average, everyday face of mental illness looks like your neighbor, your supervisor, your child's teacher, like me. I thank God for the social worker that was staffing the ER that evening. She used her knowledge of the system to necessitate a full mental health assessment for me and advocated through the wee hours of the night to secure me a bed in a hospital. She saved my life by demanding that those who were tasked to serve me, did their jobs.

Once my bed was secured, I took a long ride up the freeway to a psychiatric hospital. It was a long ride because: 1) the damn EMT person was trying to chat me up with small talk (um, I just had a breakdown; not interested in what college you're going to!); and 2) no hospitals in my home county would give me a bed. Again, because I wasn't suicidal enough. Arriving at the hospital, still shaking, terrified I made a mistake, I couldn't have been more ashamed.

COMMITTED

My first encounter was an act of kindness I'll never forget. The welcoming committee in the form of a young man whose face was covered in wounds; some healing faster than others. His eyes were sad and wild and tender. He introduced himself and extended his hand. I told him my name.

"You're going to be ok," he said. "We take care of each other here. The first couple days are rough but you're gonna be fine."

As I sat there, the staff whizzing past me like I was invisible, I wondered if I was on the wrong floor; so many young faces. How had they become so sad and so lost so early in their lives? So many scars on their arms and faces.

Someone came to say they would admit me, and I followed them to a room tucked behind the reception area. I was told (not asked) to disrobe for a skin test. Huh? The strip search was masked as "skin test." Naked, cold, monitored, questioned. I immediately wondered what had I done to myself?

I was given a hospital gown and plastic slides. I was given a large laundry basket with the clothes I had originally had on, and my backpack. They had to go through everything and clear it as "safe." That meant they took the strings out of my favorite sweat suit, took my tennis shoes (because of the laces), and put all my toiletries in a smaller plastic bin. After confiscating my phone, they took an inventory of everything and ran down the rules. "You must get approval to…" was pretty much the beginning of every sentence.

There is far too much overlap between prison and the psychiatric hospital. Far too many choices are taken away. Very basic choices. They are all under the premise of keeping us patients safe; but the execution is punitive, humiliating and dehumanizing.

The following day was my first family visit. My beloved brought my mother and father, divorced for decades now. I know the news of my illness meant they would want to see me. My wife also knew there was no way to come visit without them tagging along. God bless her for bringing them because I know the two-hour ride up there could be its own short story.

They could not have been more uncomfortable. My father couldn't help but try and make jokes, saying he wasn't sure if they were going to "bring me out in shackles or what, hee hee." I'd literally never seen my mother smile so much. She ain't never been the smiling, open-armed mama that got a pot of something for you when you come home. But the emergency of my "crazy," and her orientation to present well, meant she showed up color coordinated, smelling good, and smiling – even here in the day room at the looney bin. Awkward doesn't begin to describe it. The last time we had all been together was on my wedding day for God's sake! Oh, did I forget to mention that my wife and I were still newlyweds when I went to the hospital? Yep, the timing was impeccable, uncanny and just Tyler-Perry-tragic.

In the true spirit of a travel guide, here are the tips and tricks to a "successful" stay in the psych ward:

Tip #1: Find you some friends

I engaged in lively hip-hop debates with an aspiring computer programmer who was legally blind. He said he didn't like Wu-Tang! If I hadn't been sedated, we might have come to blows. He made cognac recommendations for me to take home to my partner, and when I earned cafeteria privileges, he was my tour guide.

While I appreciated this young man's hospitality, my main man was an older brotha I spotted during dinner. Out of respect of all I had been taught, I approached him to see how he was, and ask if I could get him anything. Psych ward be damned, I respect my elders. Salt and pepper beard, and working with

half a mouth of teeth, this cat was still kind and cool. His
housing had been abruptly taken away and he became depressed
and a danger to himself. He went on and on about his best
buddy, Boss Man, a chihuahua who was being cared for by a
friend. He adored Boss Man; the dog was all he felt he had left
to live for.

Tip #2: Concede without thought or expectations; privileges are everything.

Wait patiently in the med line. It's easy to forget you
have nowhere to go and get restless holding on to the
entitlement to good customer service that you had outside.
Don't.

Read a book, color something; there are tons of colored
pencils and crayons around there.

Points are everything. More points, more privilege.
Group therapy is more a concept than a reality. However, when
you attend (despite involvement), you get points. So, completing
the worksheets on self-destructive behavior and enduring that
snotty-ass intern seems your only choice if you ever want to
access the only real coffee and creamer in the joint.

Tip #3: Take care of each other

The staff protect themselves with a special brand of sterility. They will not see you because they don't want to. So, you must advocate for each other when necessary because they don't want to cause a ripple effect of agitation. Examples of acts of collectivism in the psych ward: swiping extra cranberry juice for Randy from the snack shack; trading strategies to appease the psychiatrist on duty; Playing 2 Chains for a wild man who, for whatever reason, found immense joy in trap music. He grooved in his night gown, with one foot covered by a dingy sock, the other bare. We also treated him to a manicure during group. He only stayed still long enough for four nails to be painted but whatever, the basic act of kindness helped soothe him, if only for a short while.

There is a kinship, a shared but familiar dread, among the group. And we know that those tasked with our care are driven by compliance rather than care. So, if we don't give each other a laugh or two, who the fuck will?

Tip #4: Some shit never changes

When Black folks find each other, especially in spaces not originally meant for us, the familiarity and relief you feel can be magical and instantaneous. It is a sweet and unique form of agency to be one of two or three Black folks in a space of very White norms. To spot your people is to grab a lifeline of our total control, and so painfully few things are under our total control. The places I am referring to are institutional in nature and therefore mimic the orientations and overall objectives of slavery: schools, banks, government buildings, DSHS, public housing. This force is what drew me to my elderly BFF; caused us to always know where the other was; check on each other in group settings. It was instinct, and I was enormously grateful for it.

On the flip side race relations in the psych ward didn't differ much from day to day life on the outside. You are still initially invisible to White folks until they feel safe. And I'm talking about staff and patients. You still feel the eyes of cliques as you happen upon the day room for group; still feel yourself passed over as someone desirable to sit next to; doctors and nurses still ask for clarification if you make reference to cultural norms during intake or check in's. And once you explain, they just say, "hmmph," and scribble a note on to the clipboard.

DISCHARGED

Discharge was sweet and paralyzing. I had no less than forty pages of forms I had signed to disavow my suicidal thoughts, but also document that should I have them, I agreed to follow the listed steps before I attempted to kill myself. Said steps included provider and crisis line phone number, deep breathing, visualizations, journal entries, approved medication, even drawings I made during group. I left in my favorite gray sweat suit, the pants loose since I never got the strings back from when I checked in. The buddies I made hugged me good bye. I gave the pregnant girl my lotion because she said she loved how it smelled. I wanted to skip and run out, but that of course wasn't allowed.

My beloved and my bestie waited for me down in the lobby. We celebrated with egg rolls and libations because that's what your girls do when you make it out of some scary shit with most of your heart intact. I never want to return because I can see how the longer some stay the worse they get. Every overscheduled, overmedicated day siphons more and more hope from you. You are in a parallel universe where success is pudding for dessert and permission to attend movie night. I never went outside once while I was there. I slept a ton, but I never got any rest. My souvenirs are a stack of forms and beaded bracelet I made (red, black and green of course). And I suppose I got a deeper sense of self that we often do after travel; a knowing that a walk in the wilderness won't kill me; that I am the source of my own health and home.

"Black Boy Joy" (2017). Watercolor, magazine clippings collage on canvas.

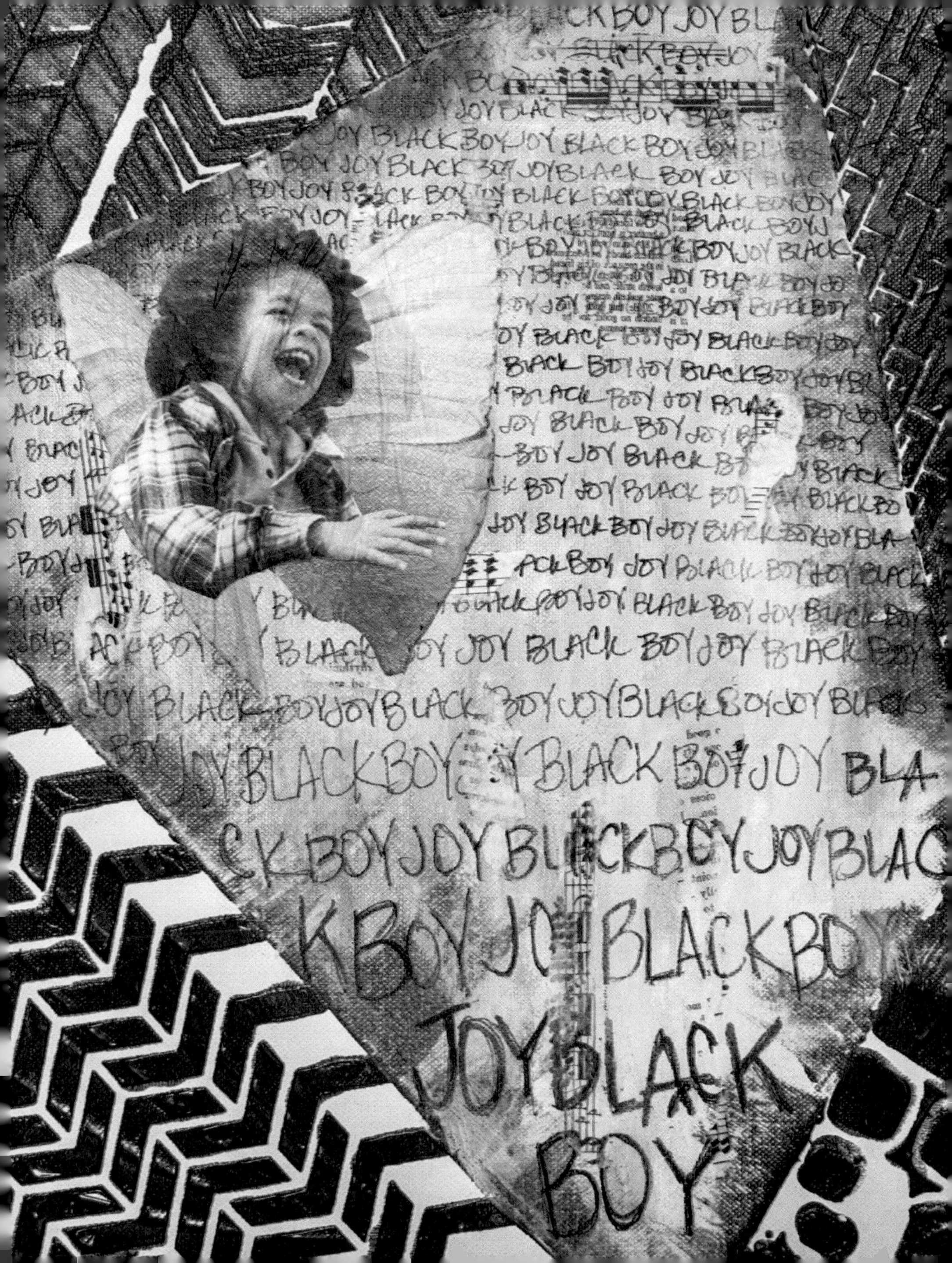
JOY BLACK
BOY

Sick

I.

A room of muted colors
and diminished efforts to be
like the others.

Throaty laughs turn ticks to tears,
checks never balance what's amiss

The scales always tip
toward the impossible question that
you can never ask.

We are the prototype for lost
but we keep looking –
        in the plastic mirror,
        in the dead eyes of helpers,
        at today's schedule of stabilization –
there is no healing here.

We are a parking lot of transgressions
that bled too much in public.

II.

I'm still sick.
I was shaken. Again.
Lulled awake by
a shallow, desperate frequency.
Jerky mind state of memories and alphabet stew.

Hollow and circular word waves
while others are at peace.

Record. Repeat. Replay.
Run. Bleed. Stay.

Little bags take up space
on my little lying face
so it's

Cold spoons and concealer
Sassy earrings, slick fedora,
Rings that divert even my attention.

Caffeine in a hip hydro flask
Don't forget lipstick.

Pay attention.
Chase invention.

Plan the mission.

Worship every detail,
EVERY detail.
Buff each one til it
shines in the light
of the sun
of the sick and sticky
world you build
every night
pebble by tile
by brick
by blood;

conceding to the ritual
because against this
I will not win.

because mine is
not a game
but a resonant condition

because I went on
and married
friction to fend off
sterile smiles

And...

I wonder what
better really looks like.

Alone

I am sure I'm not the only one
orbiting routine and ritual,
wings heavy with
migratory patterns vibrating blue,
summoning multiple suns
to burn straight through me.

I am sure I'm not the only one,
to curse hope for lying
about the goodness of people
when darkness of division
snatches a black girl back
from believing in yes.

I am sure I'm not the only one
to lose my mind,
lose my life, waiting to die
at hands trained by
shield and siren,
caseworker, pusher.

I am certain
I'm not the only one.

Clear and Present Anger

Stop smearing me across your fists
and calling it affection.

Let me get to the work
of turning this tornado
into the notion that

I am my most suitable lover.

Stop searching my body
for traces of your soul.

Release yourself
from the lie
that love is a long game
of chess and suffering.

I am divine mystery even as I weep.

Stop eating my heart for breakfast
to fill the hole in your own.

Yours is not
the only home I've known;
there is no fear in
a life without you.

Search

Time is a landslide
that clobbers you like an elephant

on greased roller skates.
You were so busy surviving

the only memories you made
make you hate yourself.

There is always a seed
under the rubble

prepared to change the course
of the whole blasted saga.

Hold your breath
and find it.

Search
until you find it.

Spring

Spring is different in the city;
still holds you sweetly
in bright budding palm,
feathered fellows serve up
the dawn chorus
and earthy strokes of grass
frame morning walks
to the bus stop.
But tension
also rises with day and
possibility is dictated
mandated and groomed
for immediate removal.
Most of us push
alongside it 'til our
transfers expire and
stock the icebox with
hog cheese and pickled peppers,
flavors and folly that make babies
and fuel fights
quenched by tall cans
and staining shaved ice.
City spring breathes
deep into me;
just a fine ass flirt.
She shucks and jives me
into believing
in me again.

Avery Young Loves Me ... He Just Don't Know It Yet

I am looking at Avery Young.
I am looking through Avery Young.
I am looking around Avery Young.
I am looking inside Avery Young.
He is akin to Baldwin and his brown boots shine.
Visceral, brown sugar laugh wakes me,
wraps me tight.
He looked at me.
Avery Young looked at me. 13 times. I counted. In hash marks.
In my journal while I wrote this. As he's talking. Blessing
strangers with literary missions
to clear their ways home.

The tables in this room, the 4 tables in this room:
Round, silver, swirly... 4 metallic mini ice rinks where us Blacks
rarely go.
But we will go. Me and Avery. Avery and I.
We'll ice skate across these silver tables
carving words of wisdom and revenge
across these tables.
We'll skid at an angle and spray these concrete walls
with the blackest, bluest joy –
the stuff of defiant conviction
and fevered embraces unbroken

by tidal waves or rusty shackles,
or steel bars or that *awful*
cunt teacher who called you dirt,
or side eyes in corner stores
or the salty blood of busted lips,
or hymens torn open by rabid hillbillies
or teddy bear shrines where our blood stains the sidewalks
or mama's wooden spoon on that ass
or daddy's ghost sneaking across town
or my lying past
or their demands that our backs crack and break
so they can smile, all the while, while we on trial.

Avery and me? Shiiiiiiiittttt!
We are shaking and spraying down all that shit!
Me and Avery!
Avery and I!
Well, truth be told
he doesn't actually have my number.
But I hear him call
from the coldest wind
from hot heads of heated debate
from the back of my dry throat
the rise in my tone
that calls my son higher
and black belly laughs
that slam bones

and cut the cake in eighths
instead of quarters
so we can all have some.

I got his messages
and wrote them on post it notes
to pepper the halls of my soul,
to light my way
from fallen to fierce.

Remember

Remember that time we won?
The time our hearts burned light and bright,
Toothy smiles left and right?

You remember?

Recall with closed eyes
the rush of warmth
from root to tip.

We were high
high on our humanity
because for once,
just once,

us was just right,
and so ripe
for peace,
peace within reach.

There was no delineation
between shades or generation,
no point to argue,
no game to win.

We were the glow, the thang, the stuff,
of a Nairobi skyline.
The breath of a baby –
soft, celebrating, sweet.

Think back to the day
we were luminous,
reflecting only the glory
of each other
just as we were –
exactly as we were!

Remember?
Breathe in and remember
that time we weren't compared
to anything but elevated!

We were relished, cherished, lauded, adored.
Welcomed with miss may auntie uncle
jelly jar rocking chair front porch greetings.

We were the standard!
We were the front AND the center,
orbited by planets
who never learned
to taste our greatness
without choking on their fear.

Looky here,

remember the altar?
The offering prepared by hardened hands;
who now know better –
the gifts of art and adoration,
honey laced, swag-filled and knee-deep dope.

Can you recollect the colors of our jubilation?
The insignia that let 'em know
we were winners,
lush and ornate,
like James Brown's cape.
We were blooms of the same garland,
the stars of the parade

And when we sang!
When we cried out in relief,
because there would be
no more retreat –
only joy.
Evoke this feeling when we meet
across the ocean or the street,

do you, will you
remember me?

Love Wins

The dead man says comparison
is the thief of joy
but just this once
look to your left

then your right.
Extend your unsure hand
behind or in front of you
to FEEL your way;

to wrestle
yourself free
from the assumption
of your unique misery.

Surmise yourself silly.
Lift the veil.
I hate to ask
but you just must.

Advancements
may deem
the human condition
more complex,

oh but baby!
I assure you
there is nothing
new under the sun.

We didn't invent or prevent
any breaking news:
an era catches fire
as two spirits,

two-spirited,
stunned by
stinging secrets
find each other

and another. And another.
Despite days
devoid of plenty
there is abundance.

I am full.
We are right-minded
at our smallest
before, between

and because of

Sister's wrath.
Father's sin.
Mother's fear.
Teacher's hate
Pastor's lust.

A fury of soul claps
in hidden hallways.
Hungry tongues
are born at moonlight dances
and coffee dates.

Our love fits and flourishes
and sometimes, we get stung
but our love
is not a punishment

Not one of us
is being punished.
We are waves,
soft, frantic
dependent on tides
and laws laden with
sloth and gluttony.

We are dancing anyhow.
No matter what.

Our dogged breath endures
our mouths recycle
demands of decency
from satellite gatekeepers.

We force their hands
to open doors
to life
to love
to joy
to freedom
to choice
to agency
to us
to them and him and her, and you.

And because of love
we always win.

"Brown Girl Dead" (2017). Watercolor, tissue paper, magazine clippings, found items collage on canvas.

A BROWN GIRL DEAD

With two white roses on her breasts,
White candles at head and feet,
Dark Madonna of the grave she rests;
Lord Death has found her sweet.

Her mother pawned her wedding ring
To lay her out in white;
She'd be so proud she'd dance and sing
To see herself tonight.

1925